LIFE TINCTURES

Conceptualized by Garima Khandelwal & Shabdanchal

Deepjoy Subba

Khirawadhi

Manpriya Dhanju

Munazza Ara

Navya Immidisetty

Parita Makwana

Pragya Maheshwari

Rashmi Sarda

Varshi Pidugu

Yash Singhal

HATCHEGG PUBLICATION

INTRODUCTION

Name: Deepjoy Subba

Place: Currently Residing in Tezu, Arunachal Pradesh

Born: on 14th of April, 1995

Occupation : Student of Bachelor of Fine Arts

(Rajiv Gandhi University, Itanagar, A. P.)

If I could give something back to the mother nature I shall give everything. I am a learner and trying to learn new things in new places. I try to compose feelings and emotions in canvas since I am a student of painting but I also, seldom, compose them on paper with my quill and ink. For me poetry is itself a language and it just needs a connection between two noble hearts to understand the feeling without even meeting and conversation. For me poetry is a result of pure honesty and it can't be 'produced', it is composed when someone is in pure and honest state, that is why I don't often compose them since human cannot remain pure and honest all the time. What I write is highly subjective but I shall be happy if someone reads them and like them even only a bit.

Sonnet- the Eighty-one

Thou like eighty-one days of melting snow
Perpetually clustering with thy blood, vein
Inside 'tis melting and penetrates now
And goes inside your friend, a man

Must have happiest the world this day
When the child in the embrace of mother, giggled first
The chilliness of chaos and misery flew away
By fulfilling thy parents' love thirst

I wish to adore thee, O benevolent since when
Thou accepted as a mate in thy life
Sure the adrenaline rushing with the level of heaven
By getting consecutive poking of sweet knife
Thou shalt live a life like an emancipated dove
With me, surrounded by the whole who shalt love the
love.

Before The Rain Comes

Behold! Here falls the first droplet of heaven
Indeed, which is not that freezing but cold
Fetch the hanging socks and the purple cardigan
For thou the wind is storm and drops are bold

A shooting gust is kissing thy bare skin
Along with the heaven's dew gradually falling
Fortunate are the drops, touching thy glossy chin
With a sudden immersion of thunder and showering

By seeing the most alluring view of nature
With a colour of grey and uncolored droplets
The sunshine smiles at her ludicrous gesture
Thy clothes await thee to be put in the caskets

Way beyond infinitude of imagination to touch thyself, O
fairy
Hope to kiss thee by the help of showering bliss and
merry

O, Viridian Mother!

Ever wonder how a child cracks laughter?
Ever wonder how a waterfall roars?
All are us and us are of our nature
Who nurture us, protect us
from every evil outside us and inside?
It renunciates to sustain the 'us'
By the river fly with an eagle
For you have the greatest will she carries
O come, the lofty cliffs and eerie breeze
Soothe me, soothe every being
Who seeks to survive
For nature who can make us
And also break us
To mother nature

A poetry on thee

I have never touched a tender flower
But I know, without touching, thee
My elevated anger of feeling, glee
I no longer a wordsman, more a plant like a clover

Since words are merely an expression
An expression of feelings I no possess longer
Thy tender heart is nor of a friend nor a lover
Thy presense is like a fairy mother

I shall never consider oedipus complex
Despite being swooned by mental consummation
Thou art a gift, a warm gift to everyone
A gift can't be possessed but makes proud

I ask not for anything but ask like a satan, a trade maker
I shall look after thy little girl (soul) without having her

Shadow (A Sestet without the Octave)

It doesn't discmrinate what we are by look
It enhances the physicality and stretches us
Many things to gether from this dark walking book
Yet we are, and so forth shall be, walking without any care
A shadow is all we possess and ought to be proud
Since it is the only clothing we brought
from godly abode and shall take with us back

Slumber Sublime

'twas like the fragmented Xanadu story of Coleridge

Someone heard me whispering melodies

Greeted me with a warm incredible kiss in my dream

I don't know when it came and came it when

Singing 'long with her in a romantic dreamy bridge

With only acquaintances of noble souls and composed
bodies

I enjoyed singing and she delighted in my vocal
melodious cream

Since I was in nature's lullaby, my dream had to be
broken

Let's Fall in

Let's not worry for the hope of tomorrow
Let's not worry for the rush of today
Let's not care for what we are not now
Let's not care what we shall be somehow
Let's be positive and perceivable to execute
Let's fall in love for (an) the eternal flute*

Let's not be perplexed for the upcoming consequences
Let's just dump the worries and break their pangs
Let's just play like cubs in the swamp of grasses
Let's just give delight to the millions of li'l heart masses
Let's try to be silvery** honest than the golden***mute
Let's fall in love for (an) the eternal flute

Let the shower of virtue and wisdom embrace our soul
and mind
and let's better choose for piercing truth rather than the
deceptiveness of kind

Cosmic Horror

The power of existence is such
We, uncertainly, know who we are
Yet unknown to the unascertained vastness
The enormous black and calm vaccum

Our vanity is such we just munch
For we know how phenomenal we are
Yet uncanny to our senses, the craftiness
The expansiveness of the stupendous
sleeping room*

We are trivial without any sanity and hunch**
Still intoxicated and drowned in pride we are
Yet we utter the morality of vacant augustness
The gargantuan appetite of human who art marooned

Cosmic horror is a reality we never did ponder
Cosmic horror is the duality we, creature, must wonder

let us Go Back

Walk and talk, o mighty lads, walk and talk under the
moon
For we have time for now and we shall, certainly, croon

Man-made paths have bored us a long time, making us
forlorn
We shall scrub* this grey serpent and better be reborn

As we are, now, escorting each other and becoming
ushers
The silver** is shying and hiding behind the light
crushers***

Now we have crossed the stingy and sharp long grasses,
we hear moaning of the stream

We trudge towards the magical yet very unembellished
sound of stream

We see now no stream but animal cry, we accompany
them by chanting and mumbling

We cross down a dried trench and many hard tablets
rumbling

We, ultimately, feel chill of going to go home and see
familiar faces

Reached the town, O lads, but the air's filthy let us walk
back by the memorable traces

Seven and Seven

Pride came to me as a sweet friend, I welcomed
Followed by Envy, who was very wilful
Gluttony was already here inside my home
Now my greed gradually grew like an infant
It was Lust, though, who forced me to do unthinkable
Sloth, after that, impelled me to do nothing
But amongst them Wrath brother was stronger, awefully

I was doomed now and gave my soul, to un-awakening
But here came some of my virtuous friends to me, same
evening
Humility came to me as an amicable girl, I un-shunned
Followed by Kindness who asked me to be helpful

Temperance was active and wanted me to freshly perform

And Charity wished to join me if my beside was still vacant

Chastity showed her graceful dance and was irreplaceable

And Diligence helped me to arrange the table and something

Ultimately, we ate our supper in merry with patience, the night went cheerfully

INTRODUCTION

I am Khirawadhi and I am an IT working professional.
I like to read books, a lot and I find peace in writing
where I can let my emotions fly.
I am a Big Manga and Anime fan.

Love in the Pandemic

It all started at the beginning of March,
Covid and our Little Romance.

Somewhere in our Random and worried talk,
You become my March Song.

While everyone was busy panicking,
I was little falling in Love and intimacy.

How can I forget that instant spark?
Strangers become lovers, while apart.

Sleeping Wrapped up in the soft pink rose petals,
Gaining weight by eating all the Ferrero chocolates.

Those 4 lucky plants which you share,
Telling me, I'll there, like 4 seasons in the year.

How I met your Father

It was the google meet, and he talks a lot,
Thinking why did I meet, but he was kind of hot.

I'll be telling stories to our kids, How I met your Father,
Talking till 4 in the mornings without getting bothered.

Dancing to love songs, during the video calls.
Getting attached, didn't know he was that tall.

Limiting ourself within that 13-inch Mac screen,
Like a roller coaster ride, we were designing our dreams.

Curiously Sharing songs on YouTube and Spotify,
While we were thinking of Netflix and the chill nights.

Talking about fantasies and what we'd like to do,
Checking out the 3 options before we say I Do.

Like a blessing

It was the final call before giving up,
Because I was frustrated and weak after getting dump.

Like a blessing you come into my life,
When I was begging God to save me before I take the
knife.

It was not me who I wanted to kill,
It was the feeling inside which need to heal.

I was living my life, making little impact on to the world,
But nobody knows, how I sold my soul.

Giving me hope of the future and holding me tight,
You always convince me, and it feels so right.

Maybe God was preparing me for this life,
Because you are an Angel, one of a Kind.

Next to Me

Him

One day I am going to wake up and see,

There you will be lying next to me,

I'll open my eyes, pulling you closer to my side,

Grinning, feeling proud, because you're mine.

As I was waiting for you all these days,

I belong to you, which I can finally say.

Her

Tomorrow, I am going to wake and see,

You are sleeping soundly, lying next to me,

As tears are rolling down my face,

I will join my hands and pray.

As I fell in love with you,

Long before I say, I Do.

If we could

If we could stay like this, can we stay forever.

Running around like a kid in the house.

Making friends with cat and roar meow.

Introvert hitting awkward when strangers around.

Feeling ourself with burgers and fried, hitting that jazz
loud.

Chasing after our dreams not people's whereabouts.

If we could stay like this, can we stay forever.

Dancing in the rain and do not cry.

Going to the spontaneous trips and never asking why.

Looking into the food blogs and giving them a try.

Working on that Tech project, wanted when we were
child.

Understanding the space but walking together the
thousand miles.

Old School romance

In a world full of Casual sex and hookups,
Fling and temporary romance.

I am looking for the soul connection.

Drive in the midnight to a 24*7 café.
Writing letters even with the tech in hand.
Teasing each other in family function.
Building a life to be proud of.
Playing Pokémon even when we are old.
Cuddle into those winter nights.
Counting freckles and grey hairs.
Making fun of our grandkids.

Poet

He writes his poems,

Like he is making love to her.

Intense gaze onto the cavity,

Like he penetrates deep inside her body.

Moving brush on the empty canvas sheet,

Like he is exploring every inch of her from hair to the feet.

He writes his poems,

Like he is bringing heaven to her.

He writes his poems,

Like he is making love to her.

Gaze

Watching your every single little detail,
Your soft little lips,
Your deep forest voice,
How your cheeks turn red,
How your eyes shine bright.

And the fact I just can't say it out loud,
I am too shy and I can't even deny.

And the fact that I just can say it out loud,
I am too proud to say that You're mine.

If I can gaze you now, I'll gaze you forever.
If I can love you now, I'll love you forever.
If I can give something, I'll give you my trust.
If I can make something, I'll make you my world.

Through Poem

You will be able to tell them through the poems,
Emotions too difficult to express, will come through.

You will be able to tell through the actions,
Love too difficult to show, will reach through.

You will be able to tell through your life,
Dreams too difficult to reach, will live through.

Clear and loud

Down Down Down !
Rain is pouring down.

Just like the rain,
Let it all out.

You are here far too long,
Filled up lungs wants to shout.

Absence of his love,
You finally hit the ground.

Rhythmless beat in heart,
Doesn't know how to make a sound.

Lost in the chaotic thoughts,
Asking where I am right now.

But somewhere in between,
You want to be heard, clear and loud.

INTRODUCTION

My Name Is Manpriya Dhanju

I Am Student of Bsc Final Year

I Started Writing Motivational Quotes In 2017

Then I Joined Mirakee App In 2018

This Is My First Time Writing Poems

These Poems Are Basically On My Life Experience.

My Dreams Vs Their Hate

I had a hold on my dreams
Since I was young,
Had a belief in myself
Going through the situations that were junk,
They tried to knock me down
Each and every time and
Thought I was sunk,
But I had a hold on my dreams
As I was stubborn,
This made me so ardent,
To achieve the goals
I had in my life's trunk.

My Imaginary Love

Over the days and Over the nights

I still thought of you,

Finding me in strenous state

You would come and rescue,

Together as a match

We will make some traitors suffer,

And there we are

Making some antagonists hate us,

But you my love makes me feel absolute

Living life with you is my resolute,

Then I arouse leaving behind the dreams of my love

As I turned back into the reality of my bad luck.

Being ME

Being 'ME' is my superpower
Being 'You' is your superpower
Let my smile spread some love
That heals everything above,
Yet again my superpower discern
As I forgot about others aversion
My self-confidence makes me the best
To demarcate me better than the rest,
Why to compare 'you' and 'me'?
When I know my qualities are better than thee
My intelligence makes me definite
For those who are still ignite.

Go on And Love Yourself

Go on as long as you reach great heights
Believe in yourself and never feel deprived,
Make yourself feel special
Let others call it self absorbtion
As you are not here to work according to their
proportion,
Go on and do what you like
Leaving others concern way behind,
Love yourself and speak yourself
Consider this the agenda of your life.

She ...(A Warrior)

She doesn't express the pain but she feels it,

She doesn't cry on it rather comes over it,

She accepts everything with a smile,

She is quite yet fierce,

She is not a mesmerizing doll

But a warrior,

She is woman

Strong enough to face every challenge.

Crack Down (Live It Or Leave It)

That's It ....

Live It Or Leave It

Heart gets hurt,

Then hurt the sadness,

When broken into pieces

Collect them and make yourself up,

Heart is filled with miseries

Shatter it out and take in satisfactory,

Why to be filled with undesire

When you know you are such a bonfire,

When disappointed then kill it

Don't be in midst of something

Live it or leave it.

Life – A Beautiful Journey

LONG ROADS ...

Though difficult to cross

Though difficult to assign,

Hesitates at first

Then becomes a feeling of exploit,

But once crossed

Gives memories of life time,

Many hurdles lies in the trial

Yet a battle to win for self –desires.

Alone

Standing in the midst of crowd
Still feeling alone,
When nobody likes you
Just become self-adored,
Solitude is depressive
But still gives paix,
It's the other way of God
To give you some life's taste.

A Friend In Mask

Not so far,

Not so close,

By my side

OR

Still apart,

Had ever known you?

OR

Still something to know more

Who are you ?

My best friend

OR

A Friend in mask.

INTRODUCTION

Hey beautiful readers,

I am Munazza Ara. I am 24 years old and a student of English Linguistics. Currently, I am doing M.phil from NUML Islamabad, Pakistan. I am a resident of Islamabad, Pakistan. I am extremely thankful to "Hatchegg publications" for providing young writers like myself, a platform of recognition. Such platforms are extremely needed so that young writers can get their work published and their talent gets highlighted. I believe that a pen is like a magic wand and with it's power I transfer my feelings on a paper. There is a famous quotation by C.S Lewis which says that " you can make anything by writing it". So this is the power of a writer who not only entertains by dressing emotions into words but also create a mirrored pool where a reader can reflect their own sense of imagination.

Here, I have compiled some of my creations that I wrote in the moments when nothing else could work to ease my mind accept writing it down. So, this is my piece of advice to all of you that whatever you think about your surroundings, write it down.

Fly

Stand up, dust yourself off,
Open your wings, flap, fly
Be fearless, be fierce, fly
Forget about the barriers
Because you are a warrior
Mark the heights of the clouds
Make the stars your shroud
Never let the crows and rooks
Lose your track of the flight
For, your destiny is the Sky
And to touch it's Light.
Get ready to fly, to glide

Wonders hidden

There are galaxies still to be discovered
Some mysteries still left unexplored

There are stories still to be narrated
There are poems still left unsung

Some philosophies are yet to be proposed
There are some myths left unfolded

Some skies yet to be shown
Some beauties yet to be noticed

These wonders hidden somewhere lies
For which someone has to explore your EYES

Serve your purpose

The clouds will pass,
The fire will cool down,
The night will dress up the sun
Let this pain enter your body,
Cell by cell, atom by atom,
Everyday brings you new form of pain,
No doubt, but remember,
You are like the burning woods
That transform into coal and ashes
Can no longer be broken down nor burned
Still it has some purpose to serve
It still has got a soul if not body
You are the clouds consumed into rain
Nourishing and soothing the plants
Be like the clouds and ashes
Grant life, give nourishment, serve your purpose.

Haste

In a haste to reach somewhere,
We are racing with each other
We try to slow down them
In a haste to reach our destiny
But little do we know
The road that we embark upon
Leads only to a dead end
With no return, no re verse
not of this verse,
Not of this road

The bird of my soul

The bird of my soul encaged behind
the bars of my bones is waiting for the day
when it will be released and fly away
to touch the skies far far away

cannot hold the shackles anymore
wants to sing on a twig beside the shore
then fly like feathers of the dandelion
in horizons to re-grow from its core

She wants to breath the life for which
she was created but body never obeyed
a chance to scatter the colours before greyed
a chance to hymn the poem before preyed

The Most Beautiful Art

Emotions and feelings costumed
in a best way of expression makes an art
that makes you reach the unreachable
Touch the untouchable imagine the unimaginable
Skies and the heavens visited in a glimpse
All is done by a pen or a brush or a hand
Creating an explicit piece of art but
The art above all for me is YOU
I would stare at you, in a room full of art
All day, all life and through all ages

Insomnia

Thick lumps of clouds crystallized in my head

Blurring my vision to see ahead but pull back

Back to the mounds of dead memories

And the withered , scentless flowers over the graves of
buried dreams

I can't help but keep my eyes open to escape

the uninvited darkness

even my eyes crave for some sleep in red tinted letters.

Stories untold

(I wrote this when I was extremely devastated by child rape incidents)

Our moms never told us the stories about human monsters who do not have long teeth or red eyes or evil face at all. They just look like the uncles from the streets. These uncles beguile us with sweets, take us to the dark places and leave us to heights of pain, agony, suffering for our parents to find our lifeless cold and numb corpse. Who prey on our flesh, who engulf our dreams with every bite and rip apart our soul with every touch? Why do they not tell us such stories of the demons who pluck the flowers of their garden and crush under their feet. Who turn our cradles into coffins. Will these flowers bloom again and whisper spring? Will they be able to hum the hymns of love, beauty and chastity?

The Worst Wars

Every one of us is fighting their own war which is only distinctive of the battlefield they choose. Where, some use force while others use a discourse. However, the worst war that you fight, is the war of feelings. You won't see blood, you won't see bruises but still you feel that your body has been broken inch by inch and all that blood and bruises are staining your heart and paralyzing your mind.

* * *

Be Fantastic Realistic

Living in a fantasy world may give you a temporary escape from the weight of the world but sometimes reality hits you hard enough to stop being mesmerized by your daydreamed fairy tales. So always be a fantastic realistic, that's the power of living.

The World Under Clouds

He: I like the balls of clouds upon the sky which entice you to chase them through oceans, mountains, hills, streams and all the smooth and crusty paths of the world. They float up in the air like a cotton candy triggering your thirst with every passing moment.

She: Hmm but during this hide n seek, the moment comes when they completely alter their shape n size and even it's colour to the point that make you question your all struggle n efforts to touch them in the first place.

He: yeah so they leave you disappointed, empty handed and gloomy. Right at that moment I realize how this world works, it keeps you busy in chasing all those shinny sparkling things that are going to be vanished in the air one day. And then you are left with nothing, nothing at all. All empty all gloomy in the world under these clouds.

She : This is this world under clouds is.

INTRODUCTION

My self Navya Immidisetty. I'm pursuing my career in law (BBA LLB). I write all genres of stories, quotes, short stories. I belong to Rajahmundry which is the cultural capital of Andra pradesh. I say writing is the only way I live. I love to write.

One Day in My life

I'm Ayush, I am not much into spirits, ghots and all; But I experienced an incident in my life which I could remember throughout my life.

This incident happened after I shifted to my new apartment in New York city, I was very excited. I unpacked all my stuff and went to sleep.

That night I felt a very cold breeze around me but, I ignored it and went to very deep sleep. The next day I got up and saw a mark on my wrist. It burned a lot. so, I took some ice out of the fridge and put in on my wrist for 5 to 10 minutes. I felt like someone was holding my wrist so tightly that my wrist became all red. So, I thought to go to the doctor near by. The doctor said that it will be fine in somedays.

 When I went back to my apartment there was a note lying in front of the door saying "we are coming " I was shocked and ran inside .There were weird things happening .I was terrified

Then the next day around 11:30pm somebody knocked the door .I was already very scared because of the shadow .So I tried calling my parents they were not picking my calls or replying to my messages. I kept trying and the person outside kept knocking. so ,as I opened the door it was my parents. I felt relieved and hugged them

After a while someone asgin knocked the door when I went to open the door there were two policemen were standing and asked me if I was Mr. Ayush. I Said "yes I'm Ayush. But what is the matter?"

The policemen said that "sorry your parents died in a car crash and these are their phone and your father's wallet."

I said to policemen "no sir this might be wrong information because my parents are here with me, see" and as I turned around there was nobody. There was only a note which says "we are home"

I started crying and said thanks to policemen and closed door and ran into my room and cried all night

Now, I have normal life but, I always have a question in my mind if my parents were really there that day?

Love Nature

I spent 10 years in solitary confinement .I tried many times to strangle a guard and escape but I couldn't .I never came out of my cell .I was blocked between the four walls of room .I used to share all my feeling with the cement walls which looks very ugly .All my 10 years are passed out in my cell itself .I used to go out to exercise yard completely alone .But one day when I was there I felt like my air around is making me pressure force .I felt like I was between the 2 pillars .I couldn't even breathe .I started running to the cell before I die , because I'm feeling as if "I was having a heart attack "within few minutes I'm in my cell .I was okay again .I felt like my brain & heart were exploding .I had agoraphobia .I suffered same when I was in my shower room again, I rushed into the cell then I felt okay and I was content ,so I didn't leave anywhere from then.

Even the rays of sunlight bothered me a lot .I used to close my windows and sit in the darkness

Other confiners used to play with me .They always bullied me and tried to drag me out of the cell manytimes

Sometimes I wouldn't be given a toothbrush or toothpaste so my teeth started to rot

So I would just get the nylon out of the mattress to brush my teeth .seeing that everybody used to make fun of me

Finally I was called by the jailer to say that "My confinement was done."

By listening to that word my heart started beating a bit heavier. I was walking through the way of entrance .

Jailer opened the door and the sun beams fell on me that made me more bothered.

My parents were waiting outside to take me, they were happy to see me. We boarded the car. They were trying to speak to me and make me talk but I didn't utter a word from my mouth . We reached our home I stepped out of the car and rushed to my room with hurry and locked myself in it.

My parents were really bothered about me ,as the time passed I was habituated to stay out of the room for some time.

My parents came up with a decision to join me in college in New delhi for pursuing my graduation

Somehow they convinced me to do so....

I woke up from the nap as the train gave me a jerk, people were rushing out of it, pushing each other and I too picked my bag and walked out of it .

Vendors selling teas, children selling toys ,heavy rush were all around finally I was in Delhi. The sun was fading in the sky. I made a way out of the station

Taxi drivers crowded in front of me ,I boarded a taxi to my college hostel.

"Bhaiya , national college of engineering and technology , 126 street Delhi"

We passed through narrow and wide streets

I saw birds in the sky flying back to their nests ,the sky growing darker and the city turning more vibrant

I peeped out of my cab window ,as far as my eyes could see there was traffic .

"How much more time will it take ?"

"Can't predict the Delhi traffic "

"Huh "I sighed .

I reached my destination I saw large campus spread in 100 acres .A solar night glowing and spreading blue light in a playground a It is first day of my college .I'm very nervous, I entered into the campus and I was sitting near a tree lonely which I like the most then I heard a gleaming white smile which drawn my attention .

There is a group of girls standing nearby me then I saw a girl with very expressive eyes, adorable smile. Her eyes were filled with joy. She is looking at a tree without any distraction. I wonder how she is enjoying lonely brushing off the world.

The first day completed. But, the picture of her was captured in me. I felt like I just wanted to talk to her, ask her why and how she is so happy being alone because being alone is hell for me but she is enjoying aloneness.

On the second day, while going home, I looked at the place where she stood yesterday but no luck she wasn't there. After a few careless steps towards my home, I found her walking with headphones on. I walked as fast as I could to reach her.

"Excuse me" I said with fear in my tone. No response. Now with increasing volume in tone, bravery in heart, I said again, "Excuse me". Now it's worked. She turned. Those eyes with kajal attracted me to look into them. "Yes", she said. Suddenly I forget to ask what I mean to ask. After loads of struggle, I asked, "Can I know your name pls?".

"Harika" she replied.

"Yesterday, I saw you at that chat bandaar smiling at a tree. May I know the reason?"

She got angry. I can see it in her eye lids, they moved close to each other. She left saying nothing, putting her headphones on again.

I do not intend to hurt her but I don't know sometimes it happens. As I don't want to hurt her more, I didn't talk to her anymore but I'm following her each and every step in the college. I didn't see her involved in anybody's matters. She just came to college, does her work and goes. She comes out of the class room if she thinks she knows the subject already and believes that the lectures didn't know more than her. In break time, she used to sit on a concrete bench lonely in a garden inside the campus reading books and comics. I admire her because of her uniqueness among other students in the college.

Some people become something in our lives. In fact, everything. Few days later, one evening, I sat on a bench watching a cricket match between our department and others. Suddenly, I could feel something fell on my hair, I suddenly tried to remove it. Those are the pieces of nuts. I looked around me. Nobody is there. I looked up. I can see a nest with two small child birds in it shouting.

I started thinking why are they shouting, are they calling their parents, are they shouting without any reason and some thoughts revolved in my brain. Finally, I thought they might be shouting because they

were hungry. Within no time, a bird with something in its mouth came to nest. I am watching it interestingly, having no attention to my surroundings. I was engulfed with that scene. That parent bird started feeding the food to child birds by putting it into their mouths. I remained looking at them.

After a few minutes, Without my knowledge, I started smiling. I don't know why I smiled. Later, I realized, for a few moments, I thought I am one of the child birds in the nest and that parent bird is feeding me and that smile is a symbol of thanking my mother for feeding me and reducing hunger.

I turned around to go. I can see a face with an expression that's-why-I-smiled-that-day. The face was Harika's.

A Smile on your face gives happiness.

A Look from you will change my mood .

A Word spoken by you will steal my heart.

A Touch given by you will make me more comfortable as
if I am in mother's womb

If kisses were raindrops

I would send you shower

If hugs were seconds

I would send you hours

If smile were water

I would send you the sea

And if love were a person

I would send me

INTRODUCTION

Hello readers....I am Parita Makwana. Future pharmacist by profession. Writing is a sort of food to my soul and I feel deep connection with myself whenever I write. I love to read poems and quotes by some of my favourite poets namely Michael Faudet, Lang Leav, Rupi Kaur and the list is not ending here. I write whatever I feel and I learn from it. I have tried many different things and concepts here.

I want to thank Hatchegg Publication for giving me this chance. They have approached me through Mirakee where I post my quotes.

To share your experience after reading my content, you can mail me on: paritamakwana1615@gmail.com and I would be grateful for that. For more of my content you can visit to http://www.mirakee.com/paritamakwana

She loved in waves

It was never the same always.
Sometimes I felt on cloud
nine.
And other days were
devastated.
Once I felt like giving up.
But the sunshine you make me felt.
I always tried not to show you the wounds,
But the trust I was building for you
As I got to know you
Gradually all fell into place.
My trust for me was the only
missing part.
All else were just perfect.

They made love

They talked for hours as the part of their routine. As all the long-distance couples do. The night was getting darker but the moon was still on with the stars shining brighter that night. They laughed about the school days and shared the picture with no filters. They shared about their college crush and the blunders they made in class presentation. From college bunks to their favourites actors in Bollywood all had been discussed. The night was still young and they ran out of words but not feelings. They didn't put down the phone but waited for the emotions to come in. They gradually started talking about their fears, insecurities, strengths and weaknesses and the vulnerability was all to show. They started feeling safe and secure with each other and even closer. This is how they made a soulful love with each other.

Yours

Just do a favour to the people you
love.
Show your true self to them.
Be vulnerable.
Gradually
This will make you theirs forever.

I loved

He leaned to kiss her
forehead.
She was about to open her
lips.
He kissed her soul first.
She fell for him there.

Love her differently

They were kissing.
Grabbing each other's lips.
Got wet and nothing was stopping them.
She was ready and sure.
He denied to not make it till the day comes.
Her eyes were teary and she was feeling
blessed.

Forever

Darling, the stars are shining today in the eyes of yours
and mine.
My love is all yours and yours is
mine.
Is it for forever of yours and mine?
Sweetie, the love I cannot
guarantee.
Respect is the thing I know to keep constant.

Always

She was sad
Weeping, keeping phone
Aside
Waiting for the phone call
Which he failed to make
Opened the folder in phone
Which she saved as
'happiness'
Swiping his photos taken during video
calls.
She lived it again and again
Fell for the person a little more..everyday.

Existence

Somedays she feel like to open up as
whole.

Her mind, heart and soul.

It was a tough job.

Naked body was easy than a
soul.

Each moment was dilemma to
her.

The vulnerability was never easy for the girl like her,

Who know that the unconditional love was only
none.

Choice

Paint her thoughts with the colors of growth
You will find yourself best among the Painters.

No prediction here

To be loved is accepting uncertainty every moment.
Not your every expectations will be met
Not your every desire will be quenched
Not your every emotion will be realized
And there enters the 'growth'.
(personal favourite)

Bond

It was a fine day, a lazy one. Both were sipping tea in their couple mug in bed. This sounds romantic after 5 years of marriage. She was reading book and he was checking his emails. She glanced at him and he seemed busy. She recalled the night before this morning which was spent in his arms, in her mind. Suddenly she asked something stupid to him.

"What would it be like to you to remain distant from me?" smiled lightly.

He replied laughingly, "It would be like rice without dal, kadhi without chawal and chocolate cookies without chocolate chips."

She enjoyed the answer knowing his foodie husband would only compare something to food (his first love and it is for life) when he holds love for that person in his heart.

She further devilry asked, "What it is like to make love with me?"

He answered planting a kiss on lips and her neck, "A workout you always enjoy, eveready for and never get tired of doing, and its due to you, you stupid hottie!!"

She was sure about the very answer and planted kiss on his forehead.

Totally out of his behaviour, today he prefered to ask one to her. He started, "Hey babe, shall I ask you one?"

She was all astonished and happy so she replied with lightened up eyes, "Yes darling, you always can. I would love to answer."

He further goes like, "Imagine a situation where we are in a long distance relationship. We cannot find enough time to communicate with each other and video calls are for weekends only. And all of a sudden we got time to video call for 10 minutes in one of the week days. What would you prefer to say or share with me at that moment?"

She smirked as if she was always ready to answer this.

"I would make you laugh as much as I can." She replied with a big smile on her face.

He was bewildered by her answer and it was clearly known from his face so before he asked any further question regarding the answer, she herself continued by taking and kissing his right hand between hers.

"To see you laughing and your eyes brighter during that is the thing I think I would rather miss the most. Because you know when you laugh and smile and you enjoy the moment due to me is like the perfect and everlasting between us. I can never she this diminished between us. And yes, those 10 minutes are for me to make you feel loved, heard and stress-free and I can never run out of this and I really never want to."

From the moment she answered he had known that he got married to a pure heart, endless beauty and peace for life.

XXX

INTRODUCTION

Pragya Maheshwari is a "Master of Business Administration" (MBA) from James Cook University in Singapore and is a first-time author of this book. She lives with her family in the state of Rajasthan in India. Her favourite pastime consists of writing personal journals and composing and reading poetry compositions. Pragya has been writing for over a year now and finds solace in writing her heart out. Her compositions consist of a collection of short poems themed on nature, thrill, fantasies, emotions, and life concepts. Hope you enjoy Pragya's exciting, roller-coaster attempt to writing through her poems that have a meaning and a story!

Fantasy dreams

Imagination is utterly magical,
In a world quite fantastical,
With the potential to sprinkle,
Youth to a woman's wrinkle!
Teleport to another universe,
Or to go back in time in reverse,
Travel elsewhere with the blink of an eye,
Pretend to be a bird who loves to fly!
Daydream like no one cares,
Stare in the dark at the stars,
Fantasize into a world of spells,
To meet a Santa jingling bells!
Magic, fairies, and palaces,
Flowing through secret passages,
Being invisible for a solar day,
To know what's waiting after today!

Breezy adventures

Cycling at the beach,
Near the sea we reach,
Feeling the cold breeze,
Gazing at the dancing trees,
An enlivening experience,
With the marine co-existence!

Seated on a roller coaster,
Eyeing at the nearby poster,
Electrified for the speedy ride,
Holding handle by the side,
Panicking from the steep diversions,
Tight turns and wild inversions,
Awaiting the breezy venture,
Screaming throughout the adventure!

Clouds

Looking down the airplane window,
I saw a bunch of clouds below,
Floating in the clear & blue sky,
Resembling cotton candies I would buy,
The child in me exclaims with joy,
Recalling the exhilarations to enjoy,
Then and there I wanted to depart and fly,
Similar to how birds wing their way to gratify,
Themselves & the audience eyeing them,
Wondering how would they experience this gem,
Where they could fly magically,
Touching the hovering white cotton candidly,
Up above beautiful green meadows,
In the midst of the clouds' shadows!

Breath

A relaxing breath,
Is utterly magical,
Teleports you somewhere,
Where you feel contented,
Carefree, calm, and composed!
Once in a while,
Come to see a place,
Stationed in nature's lap,
Away from the hustle and bustle,
Of the city, people, and work,
Just to sit back and inhale,
This oxygenated bliss!
A life-giver and a portal for energies,
Inhale positive, exhale negative,
To stay zestful and remain restful!

Capturing sunsets

Whenever is the time,

You look out of the window,

And set forward to watch the setting sun,

To feel its radiating light,

Showering on the materialistic world!

'Oh my god! Look at the sunset' is the exclamation,

That wakes up your inner photographer,

Those internal grudges channelize thereafter,

Moulding positive thoughts and perceptions!

The way you look and feel the rays touching you,

Your eyes glued to the view,

There's a pleasure that runs through!

And we see you rushing out to the balcony,

Looking out for the best camera,

To capture the ethereal beauty,

And sketch out the evening bliss!

Life of a Dandelion

Born in the springs,

A green plant it brings,

That forms a tiny bud,

Growing in the fertile mud,

Reforming into a shiny yellow flower,

Adds beauty to the planet's golden hour,

Beneath those yellow grows,

There is a seed that shows,

Gradually turns yellow to white,

Petals from heavy to puffy light,

Dispersed by the winds defined,

Or blown away by mankind,

Appreciate the dandelion's sacrifice,

To fulfill their wish when they blow twice!

Tears

Whenever I feel hurt,
There are things that I avert,
Why don't humans understand,
That I belong to this land,
Pricking remarks they blurt,
Feels akin to bee-sting insert,
Rather than the admire,
They instantly set me on fire,
No matter how much I try,
It makes me reflect on and cry,
Pondering why am I so unwise,
As I write, tears roll down my eyes!

Simple things in life

Simplicity matters,
In a world that constantly clatters,
Take a walk around,
With greenery in the background,
Meditate in the air,
Free of any polluting affair,
Donate to the needy,
Without being greedy,
Dedicate time to thyself,
That will solve grudges all by itself,
Respecting others will reciprocate,
Into earning good wishes with no hate,
Smile to yourself and all,
That will make you feel tall!

Memories

Memories are the sweetest gifts,

For our mood to quickly uplift,

Recalling the hilarious minutes,

Creates a platform for us to smile,

For negativity to get out for a while,

One of the best ways to keep us alive,

To make our heart shoot up & revive,

Is to mentally travel back to the past,

Refresh all the terrific moments,

And frame them to cherish forever!

Universe and beyond

The third planet,
From the source of energy,
Stands our home: our universe,
Known for sustaining life,
Besides the other known planets,
Of each size revolving around,
In our humungous solar system!
Inclusive of comets and asteroids,
Gigantic bright stars and dark black holes,
There is an infinite expanse of phenomena,
Other than what we know and see,
Even bigger galaxies we could ever foresee!

INTRODUCTION

Rashmi Sarda is from Jaysingpur, a small town in Kolhapur District, Maharashtra. She has been writing poems as a passion. She provides poem in English language with Indian Style. She enjoys rhyming as her poem pattern. She does her writing based on the facts. She loves to play piano. She believes in her own writing skills. Her educational background is in MBA. Her writing skills may be confirmed from Mirakee application. **(@rashmisarda)**

Dreaming of future to be brighter,

Running behind for becoming writer.

Having MBA as education,

Setting up big ambition.

Always rhyme her own writing,

Thanks family for supporting.

Worldwide Pandemic Covid19

China's unwanted virus experiment,
Lead for lockdown announcement.
Avoid going out without mask,
Re-live moments with indoor task.
Social distancing from others is prime,
Teaching us to enjoy family time.
Compulsorily sanitize your hands,
Arranging marriage without bands.
Students are having loss in academic,
People are fade up of this pandemic.

Mother- A True Beauty

It's simple saying beauty lies in nature,
But for me beauty lies in my mother.
She is person always in trouble,
But yet wants to give happiness in double.
She will be in pain,
But holidays will never be claim.
She will carry all loads in the cart,
But is only person pure by heart.
She has an unique relation,
But still manages to hide every emotion.
Her blessings always shower,
Building up love's tower.
Mom is my safety zone,
As she is greatest backbone.

Independence Day Special

Let us enjoy in our kingdom,

As we have got freedom.

Let us be proud everyday,

As we have got happiness on this day.

Let us give salute to our soldiers,

As they are ready to give their lives for us.

Let us be pride of being citizen,

And proudly say WE ARE INDIAN.

Best Friends Forever

Best friends are person on whom we trust more,
And they are deep inside heart core.
Losing them will be very sad,
But being crazy with them makes me glad.
Trying to bring a little smile,
Sitting apart a few mile.
"I am always happy", they make sure,
They are medicines that make me cure.
Teasing each other we never bother,
It's cutest bond when we are together.

Dream Education

High level of studies cannot compress,

And this makes students depress.

Science, Commerce, Arts creates confusion,

Interest in subjects give solution.

Challenging today's competition,

Running behind self-passion.

Having big ambitions,

You will be a CHAMPION.

Daddy's Girl

Giving me world's pleasure,

You became my greatest treasure.

In childhood, I demanded ice-cream,

But today you are struggling to fulfill my dream.

A girl wants her prince like you,

Because your princess loves you.

You are family's pearl,

And I am proud to be DADDY'S GIRL.

Social Networking

Today's generation is social networking's fandom,
Posting pictures all random.
People search for various information,
And finds Google as every solution.
Coming across with many others,
Late night chatting never bothers.
Slow and steady making new friend,
Social networking has no end.

Home Sweet Home

Place where we spend childhood,
And plan entire livelihood.
Built with trust and emotion,
Where grandma makes lot of devotion.
Place where we get shelter,
And blessings of every elder.
In world wherever we roam,
Peace is always in HOME SWEET HOME.

Expectations

Though being hated,

Some affection is being expected.

Though being cheated,

Some loyalty is expected.

Though genders being discriminated,

Some equality is expected.

Though castes being differentiated,

Some humanity is expected.

And so expectations always hurts.

Mom to Be

Hey Beautiful Lady, take little extra care,
As little angel stays there.
This is very special and beautiful feeling,
Enjoy it with every little carving.
Keep diet routine in the flow,
Because day by day your face will glow.
One more life in you will beat its heart,
Which will soon become your new life's part.
Giving birth to little one,
Will revel secret whether daughter or son.

INTRODUCTION

HOLA ! to every beautiful soul out there reading this . Myself varshi pidugu ,a medical graduate from JIPMER,pondicherry.

Best feeling is when you cannot utter a word but can be heard .. Not everyone can express ..not everyone can tell you in a way you understand .Books have always played a role in providing solace for those who wants to be heard and giving a clarity for the confused ! A right word at right time have power to change lives .Hoping to be one of those who could give right words at right time atleast for few who needs them , here are my perspectives of some aspects in our daily life .

I dedicate this to my grandparents (GANDHAM CHANDRAIAH & SUSEELAMMA) Their love ,hard work ,discipline and care helped generations to walk in a more dignified way Anything I say is less compared to their dedication in making our lives the best .

Blessed to have my family and friends without whom my life wouldn't be so bright. A heartfelt thanks to each one of you for introducing life to me in the most beautiful way !! special thanks to my little sis priya pidugu .

Elixir That Never Worked

It's an elixir that never worked and never will
The more you take it , the more you drench in it
Drench in a world of dissatisfaction
where you will be in a haste to be happy but never will

It's an elixir of PERFECTION that
when taken will never let you sleep with content
as it makes you believe that you are not enough
for things to be perfect !!

perfection is something to be used with caution .. too less
of it maynot give desired results . too much of it can suck
out a happy and peaceful life out of you . In an attempt
to be perfect don't miss the beauty of the process .

Which Way

They give you everything

words of boldness , words of coldness

words of trust,words of insult

words of care , words of rage

words of love , words of hate

words of repair , words of despair

they give you everything

that you devoid , that you avoid

It's upto you to take those

that matter or just clutter your brain !!

people around and the world has their own way to sway you. if you just let every word, every action, every incident effect you then I am afraid if your living your life your way or their way. Always and always everything you say or do should be because you wanted to say or beacause you wanted to do it.

them wanting us to be them and us wanting them to be us is the reason for most of the chaos around. we may not change how others act or say but the way you respond is entirely your responsibility. when you have that much of stability within you, you can make best out of the worst scenario too!

Drama of Love

There is little smile
there is little wail

there is little bliss
there is little blaze

there is little like
there is little hate

there is little high
there is little hurt

there is little solace
there is little soreness

when there is little love
there is this little drama in life !!

No two of us are entirely similar . no two of us are perfect for each other . In any relation .. a mother to a child , a elder to younger , a wife to husband ..a friend to another whatever the relation is ..no one can truly fetch the other always ..no one can impress the other always . but despite all the hurt , disappointments we give , few stay with us   no   matter   how   flawed   we   are.   when we acknowledge this we will not wait to show our love to them . yes, it is complicated but it is definitely beautiful to be loved and to love !!

Welcome the Pain

pain don't go in vain

as you gain

Gain the patience

Gain the confidence

Gain the experience

Gain the courage

Gain the knowledge

Gain the spirit of living !

somehow its hammered in our brains to always look onto the brighter side , to be happy always , to never fail or fall .we are protected from experiencing pain . but I would say we should fail at least once in our lifetime. we must know the other side too to know life as a whole. this pain grounds us to the reality and gives us the platform to experience the brighter side in a more stable way . The early you experience pain, the early you know how to live. Afterall without the labour pains we wouldn't be here. take the good pain in life. That's how we grow .

Innocent Cloud

Now that I grew up in time

my story has become more like a mime

muted by knowing the real world

My visions blurred as clouds cleared

confused I am to live the sad reality

or to be happy under shade of my innocence !

If there is something thats constant in this universe that is "**THE CHANGE** " . our family , our friends , our little world thats all we know till a certain age . we know very little how the outside world is . But as we grow in time .. we will get to know that there is equal bad as good . equal hate as love . we wish to run back to our cozy little place where we didnt know this filth . but we cannot . this transition will be filled with jitters all along till we accept the world for how it is .In my opinion IGNORANCE IS BLISS ONLY WHEN WE KNOW WHAT WE ARE IGNORING BY OUR OWN CHOICE .

Lows

Live. Outweighing .Worries .Stubbornly

It's not easy to be low , it needs courage to be low

courage to wake up each day knowing

it's going to be the same as before

courage to drag your draining energy

to see one more sunrise and sunset

courage to face the gloomy clouds which

are stubborn to leave you in peace

courage to count the days for when

it will be over !!

It's not easy to be low

It's not something one can understand completely

even if you pour your heart out

It's you who are living with it

it should be you fighting to win over it

Do anything that keeps you moving

moving faster than the clouds over your head

move until the monster looses site of you

the outside world may or maynot be with you

but the one who can demolish the demon is you

not by killing yourself , but by cutting the cords
through which its feeding on you

Have ounce of courage to fight the battle
slowly maybe , but surely you will win
It,s all within you .. the magic that overrules the demon
it's only within you !!!

Definitely its not easy to be low
But it's not impossible too !!

I am glad that we are slowly giving our priority to mental health overcoming the stigma about it . Now a days we hear a lot about being depressed . Pathetically happiness is being made a unreachable destiny . If you read a text book of psychiatry i can assure there will be many things one can relate to .. Depression is true ..but before claiming to be depressed just introspect . We will be unhappy for whole lot of reasons . Crosscheck what it is ..what mistakes you have done .. Or what situations went wrong . Mostly ..if you fairly introspect you will find an answer to why you are not happy ..sometimes most of the cases it will be your own deeds ..your own thoughts that led you to where you are now ..

As a reader i would like to ask you one question

1)Is there any issue that is bothering you but you swept it under the rug ?

2) If yes , just dissect it .why and how it happened

3)If you can do something about it . Like from changing your own habits to confessing your mistakes .. Anything ... Do it if you think it ll make things better

4) If there is truly nothing you can do about what happened .change the way you see it ..see it in the best possible way you can

Accept, forgive, move on.. It is easy to say, hard to do .. But, don't you think that little effort is worth your happy life ahead. Life is really short to have regrets and anger .. If not all of it ..at least the way you see it can be changed .Do it for your own good and happiness .

Dear Empath

Live your life as others have their life to live too

fill yourself with love first as only then you can

give others from place of abundance

you can go on and keep giving but,

there will a point where you can give no more

you are capable of feeling the pain that has no origin from
you

however you take it so as to minimize theirs !!

Don't you think

you are living too much of theirs ,

leaving them too little to work on

let them grow through that pain

for they have their own life to mend and you have yours
too !!

In view of principle of moderation, I believe being too good is not soo good . Don't get me wrong !! I have seen people who can give soo much to anyone but when they need it they get too little. and by giving too much to who can actually work on it , we are compromising their potential to thrive .I am glad to see the good but if you keep giving it relentlessly somehow its value will be lost . if

you have some good .you have to protect it too ! remember
.. you can't be a ever giver it doesn't mean you calculate
and help .. be cautious of your own self needs and care.
Do not sabotage your self and prioritize others over you
for petty things . Give it to those who actually need your
care and love !

Have a great joyous days ahead
Sayonara
Varshi pidugu

INTRODUCTION

Yash Singhal

Instagram handle:- @yashsinghal7

Yash Singhal is a 21 years old M.Pharm student along with a diploma course in nutrition and health education(DNHE) from IGNOU. Apart from his profession the only thing for which he is passionate about is writing. His biggest inspiration is his father. Show some love to this debutant.

Cursed Age

I am tired of being alone
Everything What I earned has now gone
My family has lost
I am ready to sacrifice myself
Just tell me the cost
No one actually try to understand me
I have become what I never wanted to be
Stress, depression, violence, crying are normal now
All I need is love just guide me how
Spent all my life for my loved ones.
And now they are facing me with pointed guns
The only thing I keep recalling
When they loved me truly with all their hearts.

- A 60 year old man

A Poem about 'POEM'

A poem is not only a
Cluster of rhyming words.
It's like a blue sky with
Full of birds.
It takes milliseconds for a poem
To take you on another world.
Poet's emotions flow in each line.
And the prompt behind it is divine.
It's impossible for some while
Others take seconds to portray it.
Words are the best healer
It holds something for every dreamer.
Whenever feelin' down
Pour your heart out on paper
And start a fresh life from next dawn.

A Woman

A woman
What does a woman want?
It's not easy to understand her.
Before every role she plays
whether it'd be a wife, sister, mother,
friend, etcetra.
She is a beautiful and elegant soul.
A little clumsy though graceful
A little noisy outside but
Silent as night sky from inside.
What she actually thinks in her head?
Does freedom what she all needs?
She does everything for her family
But we fail to appreciate her deeds.

Miserable Life

Livin' in the same
Still so different world.
Unknowing of the amenities
Spending their lives in vain.
All the luxuries are for us
Nobody thinks about them.
Their lives holds no price
They are just meant for
Experiments just like mice
Wonderin' when will they know their power
They hold the ability to smell like a flower
Only the hardwork they know
They are poor people
Can't even reap what they sow.

Family

Family - the word itself ends with ILY
is the most precious
Gift anyone can have.
It provides us abundance
Like dove.
They are the ones who truly care
They will always be at top I swear.
I don't want my prosperity
I already owe a lot for their charity.
All the worry and stress they fade away
They love with all their hearts
Believe me it's not a cliché
Embrace their presence even if it is uninvited
In thi modern era
Keep them united.

Modern Love

Love has lost its meaning
It needs some serious screening
My heart is hopeless and screaming
But it is still dreaming.
I just want to be redeemed
Is there anyone to
Help me in finding my self esteem.
Every lonely evening
I feel like my soul is leaving
It doesn't know where it would lead
Compassion, honesty and loyalty
Is its only greed.
In this world,
Love has lost its meaning.

I'd call it a Nightmare

I saw a dream
Last night
It was dull but
Still bright
You were with me
Holding my hand
We were dancing on
The chords of our favourite band.
But the moment didn't last long
We couldn't walk along
A stranger took his entry
I wanted to protect you
like a sentry.
But you didn't want that
And left me with my bare hands.

They don't get

People force me to write
More often
They say my words act
As medicine.
But do they know the pain
Of penning the emotions.
I think it is my life's
Biggest bane.
It's painful to relive the moments
A silent heart behaves like a clamant.
But I still feel wonderful
When I write
No matter if it is against my will.

Love

The society holds hatred

Still hearts are sacred

It has the ability to love

Can be called as brave

Human beings are made up to praise

But we got into useless race

What if we become a little more loving?

Instead of being a taker, practise giving

Our basic nature is still care.

But we have contaminated our soul

It isn't fair

Let's make this world a better place

Once gone

You won't get backspace

River

Flow like a river, find your path even
From the toughest roads.
But never end into an ocean.
Live with your own Identity.